It's Not Funny I've Lost My Money!

WRITTEN BY

Melody Carlson

ILLUSTRATED BY

Steve Björkman

CROSSWAY BOOKS · WHEATON, ILLINOIS
A DIVISION OF GOOD NEWS PUBLISHERS

Published by Crossway Books

a division of Good News Publishers

1300 Crescent Street

Wheaton, Illinois 60187

First printing, 2000

Printed in the United States of America

LIBRARY OF CONGRESS CATALOGING-IN-PUBLICATION DATA

Carlson, Melody

   It's not funny, I've lost my money / written by Melody Carlson; illustrated by Steve Björkman.

     p. cm.

   Summary: a rhymed version of the Bible parable of the woman who loses one of her ten coins and rejoices when she finds it.

   ISBN 1-58134-183-0 (alk. paper)

   1. Lost coin (Parable) -- Juvenile literature. 2. Bible stories, English -- N.T. Luke. [1. Lost coin (Parable) 2. Parables. 3. Bible stories -- N.T.] I. Björkman, Steve, ill. II. Title.

BT378.L56 C36 2000

226.8'09505 -- dc21

                           00-008836

09	08	07	06	05	04	03	02	01	00
15	14	13	12	11	10	9	8	7	6	5	4	3	2	1

To the Boeshans' Kids:

Cortney, Keith, Jessica & Jameson

MELODY CARLSON

For the great teachers at

Mariners Christian School

STEVE BJÖRKMAN

Old widow Hannah lived alone in her house

Except for a dog and a bird and a mouse.

Although she was poor and hadn't a lot,

She always gave thanks for all that she got.

Now Hannah worked hard and saved every cent

In an old wooden box with a latch that was bent.

Ten coins of silver were safe in her care.

Year after year, she kept them all there.

Each day in the morning, she rose from her bed,

And straight to her box, Old Hannah would head.

She set all the coins one by one in a row,

And that's when she counted; she did it like so:

One coin buys a hammer; two coins buy a coat.

Three coins for a pair of lambs; and four will get a goat!

Five coins for a donkey; six to buy a cart.

Seven for a milking cow, and eight will buy fine art!

Nine coins are a fortune for a poor, old gal like me,

But thank the Lord, I have ten! What a sight to see!

One day before breakfast, she had quite a scare.

While counting her coins, she found one not there!

She counted once more, then said, "It's not funny!"

With a shout she cried out, "I've lost my money!"

She looked at the mouse, and he gave a shrug.

She questioned the dog, curled snug on the rug.

She shook her old head and looked all around

And said, "If it's lost, then it must be found!"

She searched in the parlor and moved all the chairs.

She dug through the closet, looked under the stairs.

She found a lost glove in the drawer that was stuck,

But in finding her coin, she was plumb out of luck.

She went to her porch and she hollered real loud.

It didn't take long 'til she drew a small crowd.

"I've lost my dear coin, and I'm in the lurch.

I need all my neighbors to come help me search."

Her neighbors all hunted, though not very hard,

Throughout Hannah's house and then through her yard.

"Hey, Hannah," called Leroy, "think—where have you been?

Then retrace your steps; start all over again."

"Good thinking," said Hannah. "A trip might just spark it!

And as I recall, I went to the market.

I'll re-walk every step that I took yesterday,

And look every place that I passed on my way."

As she walked to the market, she searched the whole road

And found a blue bottle, a fork, and a toad.

She stopped at the fruit stand and looked through the cherries,

The peaches, the oranges, the grapes, and the berries.

ithout any luck, she continued to seek

Through pitchers and bowls and a pot with a leak.

She went to the bakery and dug through the bread,

Peered 'neath the muffins, then just shook her head.

Her search appeared hopeless; it seemed time to quit.

She paused at the lamp-shop, a moment to sit.

She looked all around her, then quickly grew bright.

"Perhaps all I need is a little more light!"

She set lamps on the chairs, on sofa and table.

The dim house grew bright, and soon she was able

To see very clearly the floors and the walls,

The windows, the doors, and even the halls.

She got out her broom, and she swept all about,

And after a moment she let out a shout!

For stuck in between the floor and the beam

It glimmered and shimmered—a bright silver gleam!

And before you could say, "Jumpin' jiminy quick,"

She pried out the coin with a sharp wooden stick.

She laughed, and she danced, and she jumped off the ground.

"I thank the good Lord, my lost coin is now found."

Old Hannah rejoiced as she polished her coin,

Then called all her neighbors and asked them to join

Her for a party, to come celebrate.

They feasted, they sang, and they stayed until late.

Jesus said: "Or suppose a woman
has ten silver coins and loses one.
Does she not light a lamp, sweep the house
and search carefully until she finds it?
And when she finds it, she calls
her friends and neighbors together and says,
'Rejoice with me; I have found my lost coin.'
In the same way, I tell you, there is rejoicing
in the presence of the angels of God
over one sinner who repents."

LUKE 15:8-10